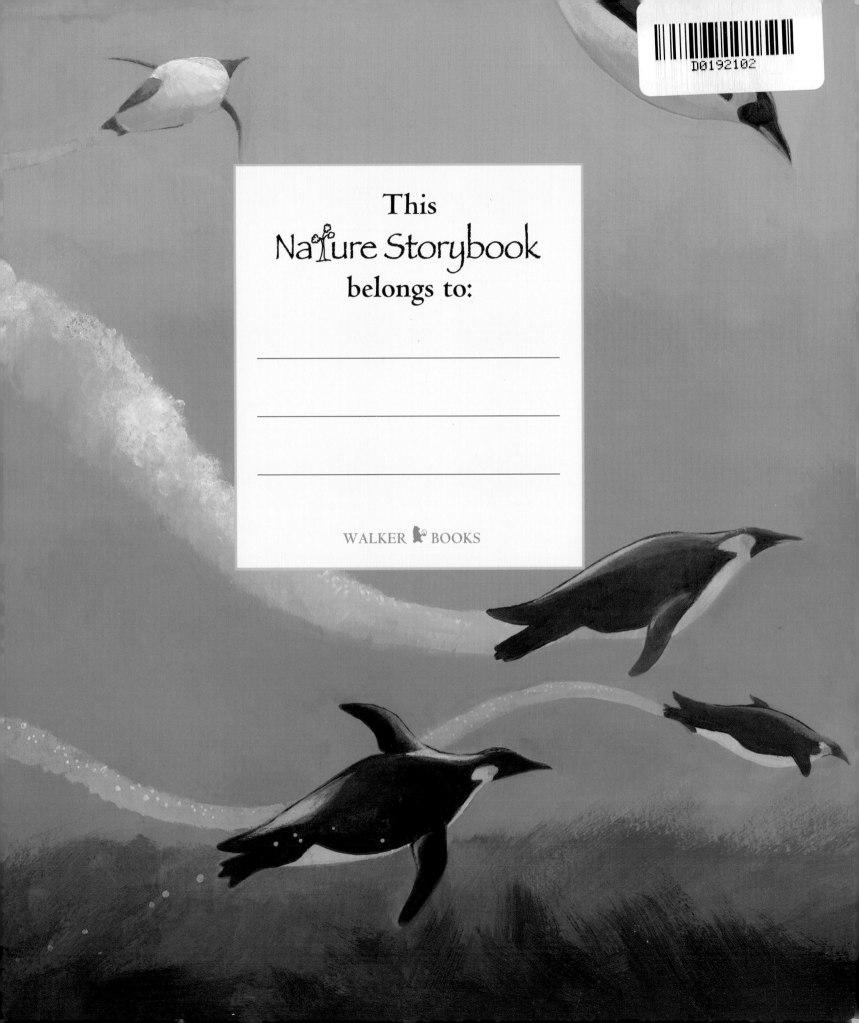

This
Nature Storybook
belongs to:

_____

_____

_____

WALKER BOOKS

There are **seventeen** kinds of penguin,
but the Emperor is the only one that breeds in
Antarctica in midwinter. The adults arrive at their
breeding areas — often as far as 200 kilometres
from the open sea — in late autumn. A few weeks
later the female lays her single egg and returns to
the sea, leaving the male to keep the egg warm
until it hatches a couple of months later.

At first the male and female take turns to look
after the chick. But soon it is big enough
to be left while both parents go fishing for
its food in the sea. By the time it's
four months old, the young penguin's coat of
fluffy down has been replaced by adult feathers.
It now also sets off for the sea,
where it has to start looking after itself.

For James, John, Steve, Tim and Tony —
and all the other dads
M.J.

For Mum and Dad,
from egg number one!
J.C.

First published 1999 by Walker Books Ltd
87 Vauxhall Walk, London SE11 5HJ

This edition published 2008

4 6 8 10 9 7 5 3

Text © 1999 Martin Jenkins
Illustrations © 1999 Jane Chapman

The right of Martin Jenkins and Jane Chapman to be identified as author and illustrator respectively of this work
has been asserted by them in accordance with the Copyright, Designs and Patents Act 1988

This book has been typeset in Humana

Printed in China

British Library Cataloguing in Publication Data:
a catalogue record for this book is available from the British Library

ISBN 978-1-4063-1301-7

www.walker.co.uk

The Emperor's Egg

Martin Jenkins

illustrated by **Jane Chapman**

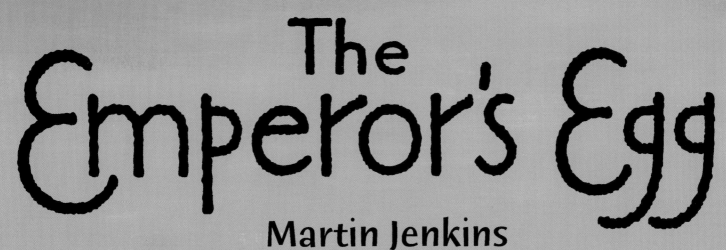

WALKER BOOKS
AND SUBSIDIARIES
LONDON · BOSTON · SYDNEY · AUCKLAND

Down at the very bottom of the world, there's a huge island that's almost completely covered in snow and ice. It's called Antarctica, and it's the coldest, windiest place on Earth.

Antarctica

The weather's bad enough there in summer, but in winter it's really horrible.

It's hard to imagine anything actually living there.

But wait...
what's that shape over there?
It can't be.

Yes!

It's a **penguin!**

It's not just any old penguin either.
It's a male Emperor penguin
(the biggest penguin in the world),
and he's doing a Very Important Job.

He's looking after his egg.

Male Emperor penguins are about 1.3 metres tall.

The females are a little smaller.